"What Do We Have for the Witnesses, Johnnie?"

Doonesbury books by G.B. Trudeau

Still a Few Bugs in the System
The President Is a Lot Smarter Than You Think
But This War Had Such Promise
Call Me When You Find America
Guilty, Guilty, Guilty!
"What Do We Have for the Witnesses, Johnnie?"
Dare To Be Great, Ms. Caucus
Wouldn't a Gremlin Have Been More Sensible?
"Speaking of Inalienable Rights, Amy . . ."
You're Never Too Old for Nuts and Berries
An Especially Tricky People
As the Kid Goes for Broke
Stalking the Perfect Tan
"Any Grooming Hints for Your Fans, Rollie?"
But the Pension Fund Was Just Sitting There
We're Not Out of the Woods Yet
A Tad Overweight, but Violet Eyes to Die For
And That's My Final Offer!

In Large Format

The Doonesbury Chronicles
Doonesbury's Greatest Hits

a Doonesbury classic by

GB Trudeau.

"What Do We Have for the Witnesses, Johnnie?"

An Owl Book Holt, Rinehart and Winston / New York

Published by Holt, Rinehart and Winston,
383 Madison Avenue, New York, New York 10017.

Published simultaneously in Canada by Holt, Rinehart
and Winston of Canada, Limited.

Library of Congress Catalog Card Number: 74-5539

ISBN: 0-03-013176-6

Printed in the United States of America

3 5 7 9 10 8 6 4

SURE YOU WANT TO MAKE THE DRIVE ALL THE WAY OUT TO THE COAST, MIKE?
OH, YEAH. I THINK IT'D BE FUN. ALSO, I'D LIKE TO SEE YOUR FOLKS AGAIN.
HEY, MA? REMEMBER MY FRIEND, MICHAEL DOONESBURY? IS IT OKAY IF HE COMES OUT FOR A VISIT?.. WHAT?.. WHY NOT?
AW, C'MON, MA, HE IS NOT... NO, REALLY, YOU JUST GOTTA GET TO KNOW HIM.. MA! WHAT AN AWFUL THING TO SAY.
LISTEN, MA! HE'S CHANGED A LOT SINCE THEN!
FORGET IT.
GBTrudeau

I'M GLAD YOU CHANGED YOUR MIND, MIKEY..
I PROBABLY SHOULDN'T HAVE. YOUR MOTHER SEEMED LESS THAN ENTHUSI-ASTIC ABOUT MY COMING.
McGovern
AW, YOU SHOULDN'T TAKE IT SO PERSONALLY, MIKE. SHE'S ALWAYS BEEN THAT WAY WHEN I BRING HOME FRIENDS. SHE THINKS SHE'S GOT EXCLUSIVE RIGHTS ON ME.
McGovern
I CAN UNDERSTAND IT, OF COURSE. I GET HOME SO RARELY I SUPPOSE I REALLY SHOULD BE ALONE WITH.. MY PARENTS.. MORE.. ..AND..
McGovern
SAY, MIKE, I WONDER IF YOU'D MIND SPENDING THE FIRST FEW DAYS IN A MOTEL?
YES.
McGovern
©GBTrudeau

NO, DON'T SLOW DOWN! HE'S **NOT** FOLLOWING YOU! JUST KEEP GOING...
I DON'T KNOW, ZONK. I THINK HE'S TRYING TO SIGNAL ME...
HE'S **NOT** TRYING TO SIGNAL YOU. IF HE WANTED YOU TO PULL OVER, HE'D TURN ON HIS SIREN, MIKE!
ZONK, I REALLY THINK WE SHOULD STOP...
BLAM! BLAM! BLAM! **BLAM!**
ZING!
ZIP!
OH, ALRIGHT, YOU WIN..

O.K., FELLAHS, SET YOUR BAGS RIGHT DOWN OVER HERE..
WHAT'S THIS ALL ABOUT? WHAT'D WE DO?
ROUTINE BORDER CHECK. JUST GONNA HAVE MAH DOG CLAUDE HERE CHECK YOU OUT... SEE IF HE SMELLS SOMETHIN' FUNNY..
SNIFF SNIFF SNIFF
HEY!... WHAT IS IT, BOY? WHAT IS IT?... YOU'RE ON TO SOMETHIN', EH, BOY? RIGHT? RIGHT?
RRR RRR RRR
GBTrudeau
J'ACCUSE!
HEY! NO WAY, MAN! I'M CLEAN!

WHATCHA GOT FOR ME HERE, JOHN BOY?
DRUGS, MOST LIKELY SHERIFF! OL' CLAUDE SMELT UP SOMETHIN' OR OTHER!
TED
TARNATION! HE WAS RIGHT, JOHN! LOOK WHAT I FOUND! A SEED!
YEP! THAT THERE'S A MARY-GEE-WANA SEED! KID'LL GET THIRTY YEARS FOR THAT!
TED
HEY! LOOK HERE! IT'S ANOTHER!.. NO, THERE'S THREE!..
WHAT! THREE? WHY, HE MUST BE A.. A....
TED
A DEALER!!
GEEZ! THAT'S FIFTY YEARS, AIN'T IT?
TED
GBTrudeau

HI YA, ZONK. HOW'RE THEY TREATING YOU?
OKAY, I GUESS. I CAN'T COMPLAIN..
SO WHAT HAVE THEY GOT YOU ON?
POSSESSION. THERE WAS SOME STUFF IN MY BAG..
WHAT? THEY FOUND DOPE IN YOUR BAG! I CAN'T BELIEVE IT!
I THOUGHT YOU FINISHED IT OFF LAST NIGHT..
ME TOO, MAN, ME TOO..
GBTrudeau

HELLO?...
HI YA, GUY! I'M YOUR BRAND NEW CELL-MATE!
THE NAME'S ZONKER HARRIS! I'M IN FOR POSSESSION OF MARIJUANA!
LUCAS. FRANK LUCAS. FIRST DEGREE MURDER.
WONDERFUL.

WELL, IF YOU REALLY WANT TO KNOW, LITTLE BROTHER, IT WAS OVER A CARD GAME..
THIS CAT CHEATED ME–BUT **GOOD!** I LOST MY TEMPER AND BLEW HIS HEAD OFF! MAN, WAS I **MAD** WITH THAT DUDE! **REALLY** MAD!
©B Trudeau
ACTUALLY, I FEEL KINDA BAD ABOUT IT NOW...
NATCH! THAT'S WHAT PRISON'S ABOUT!

FRANK, YOU EVER BEEN BUSTED FOR DOPE ?
1967
ME? OH, SURE, MAN. I GOT BUSTED ONCE WHEN THIS COP SAW ME SMOKING A JOINT IN PUBLIC!
1967
PROCEDURALLY, THAT CAT DID **EVERYTHING** WRONG! – HE FORGOT TO CHECK THE EVIDENCE, WROTE DOWN THE WRONG DATE.... NORMALLY, THE CASE WOULDA **NEVER** GOT TO COURT!
1967
UNFORTUNATELY, I WAS HOLDIN' UP A GROCERY STORE AT THE TIME.
©BTrudeau

HELLO, SON.
HELLO, POP. THANKS FOR COMING.
I.. I.. GOT HERE AS SOON AS I COULD. THE SHERIFF... HE SAYS IT'S A DRUG RAP YOU'RE BEING HELD FOR... THAT IT LOOKS BAD... MAYBE A LONG SENTENCE... I COULDN'T BELIEVE MY EARS...
YOU KNOW, YOUR MOTHER IS GOING TO BE VERY UPSET, SON..
OH, POP, I FEEL JUST **AWFUL!**
SHE WAS REALLY COUNTING ON YOU TO HELP HER WITH THE GARDEN THIS SUMMER..
I KNOW, POP, I KNOW.
GBTrudeau

SO HOW'D YOUR OL' MAN TAKE IT, KID?
REAL HARD, AMIGO. HE THINKS HE'S TO BLAME.
I MEAN, HE REALLY FEELS GUILTY! HE KEPT MUMBLING THAT THE PRESIDENT WAS RIGHT—THAT HIS GENERATION HAS BEEN TOO PERMISSIVE WITH ITS CHILDREN.
I DUNNO... I GUESS HE FEELS KINDA BAD BECAUSE HE GAVE ME MY FIRST JOINT..
YEAH? GOOD STUFF?
OUT OF THIS WORLD!

WELL, MR. HARRIS, BEING AS YOU'RE HERE AND ALL, I'VE DECIDED TO LET YOU BAIL OUT YOUR SON.
BAIL WAS SET THIS MORNING. UPON PAYMENT, HE WILL BE FREED.
HOW MUCH?
HOW MUCH YOU RECKON YOU ALL BROUGHT DOWN HERE WITH YOU?
ABOUT $1,000. YOUR HONOR..
I HAVE THE MOST EXTRAORDINARY COINCIDENCE TO REPORT.
BAD MOVE, DAD.
© GBTrudeau

WELL, OUR TIME'S ABOUT UP, SCOT, SCOT AND TED. I'D LIKE TO WISH ALL OF YOU AT NASA GOOD LUCK WITH SKYLAB.
ANS
JUNE 1
IS THERE ANYTHING YOU'D LIKE TO SAY TO OUR VIEWERS BEFORE YOU LEAVE FOR YOUR EPIC JOURNEY?
NOPE, NOT ME. HOW ABOUT YOU, TED?
NOPE, NOT ME. HOW ABOUT YOU, SCOT?
YES, I'D LIKE TO SAY HELLO TO MY SON SCOT.
© B Trudeau

TEN, NINE, EIGHT, SEVEN, SIX, FIVE, FOUR, THREE, TWO, ONE.. BLASTOFF!
.. I SAID BLASTOFF!...
OKAY, WHAT'S THE DEAL HERE?!
OOPS.. SORRY.. WAIT A SEC..
©BTrudeau
VROOOM!
THERE WE GO...

WELL, HERE WE ARE, GUYS! THIS IS OUR NEW HOME FOR THE NEXT 28 DAYS.. HEY... THERE'S SOME-THING WRONG WITH OUR BATTERIES!..
YOU'RE KIDDING! THE BATTERIES AREN'T WORKING? YOU MEAN THERE'S NO ELECTRICITY?!
LOOKS THAT WAY...
USA
OH, NO!!
THIS IS SKYLAB! COME IN, CAPE CANAVERAL, COME IN!!
SCOT! YOU'RE PANICKING, MAN, YOU'RE PANICKING!

HOUSTON?
BLEEP
WHAT IS IT, SCOT?
COULD I SPEAK TO MAINTENANCE, PLEASE?
GBTrudeau
SORRY, SCOT, IT'S AFTER 5. NO ONE'S HERE.
NUTS. I'VE GOT TO TALK TO CHRIS. WE'VE LOST OUR POWER... COULD YOU TAKE A MESSAGE?
SURE.
TELL HIM SCOTTY CALLED.

HOW ARE THE REPAIRS COMING, DOCTOR?
DON'T KNOW YET.. WITH SOME LUCK, THEY MIGHT MAKE IT..
THEY'RE GOOD MEN, DOC..
GOOD MEN, YES. BUT THEIR TOOLS?
YOU'VE GOT A POINT.
GBTrudeau
SCOTCH TAPE!
ROGER!

SAY, SCOT, HOW MUCH DID YOU SAY **SKYLAB** COST?
2.5 BILLION DOLLARS.
OKAY, LEMME SEE... IN ORDER TO JUSTIFY THAT EXPENSE, THE NINE ASTRONAUTS HAVE TO DO 2.5 BILLION DOLLARS OF RESEARCH OVER A TOTAL OF 140 SKYLAB DAYS..
THAT BREAKS DOWN TO 18 MILLION DOLLARS A DAY, OR **6 MILLION** PER ASTRONAUT PER DAY!
NO SWEAT. I ALREADY DID 2.75 MILLION THIS MORNING...
©BTrudeau
HEY! YOU DID?
SURE! I GOT UP EARLY.

.. AND MARTY AND PETE SAY TO TELL YOU THEY'RE ENJOYING CAMP A LOT!
BLEEP
UM.. THE MAN HERE SAYS WE'VE GOT TO STOP TALKING NOW.. SO I GUESS THAT'S IT..
YOU BE GOOD UP THERE, AND DON'T FORGET, SCOT... I.. I LOVE YOU VERY MUCH...
ROGER, HONEY.
BLEEP
GB Trudeau

SCOT, SCOT AND TED! WE'VE GOT SOMEBODY SPECIAL WHO WANTS TO TALK TO YOU!
THE PRESIDENT!
WE WERE HOPING WE COULD HAVE THE PRESIDENT HIMSELF CONGRATULATE YOU, BUT HE WAS A LITTLE BUSY THIS WEEK... AS WAS THE VICE-PRESIDENT...
SO, MEN OF SKYLAB, HERE TO CONGRATULATE YOU INSTEAD, TO TELL YOU HOW PROUD AMERICA IS OF YOU – THE LIEUTENANT-GOVERNOR OF IOWA!
GBTrudeau
HI YA, BOYS!...
I BET WE DON'T GET A PARADE EITHER..

USA
YIPPEE! THE CHUTE'S OUT! I'LL BET OUR WIVES CAN SEE US NOW!
USA
IS YOUR LITTLE GAL ON THE CARRIER?
NO... I THINK SHE'S WATCHING AT HOME...
C'MON, HONEY! YOU CAN MAKE IT! YOU CAN MAKE IT!
BEAUTIFUL! NOW ONE WITH THE BABY!
CLICK

BINGO! RIGHT ON TARGET!
YUP! HERE COME THE CHOPPERS!
BOY, HAS THIS BEEN SOME KIND OF EXPERIENCE FOR ME! ESPECIALLY FOR MY FIRST FLIGHT!
YOU KNOW, PART OF THE REASON IS THAT YOU TWO SPACE VETERANS HELPED ME OUT SO MUCH. I WANT TO THANK YOU FOR THAT, SCOT.
I'M TED.
WELL, YOU, TOO.

FIRST OF ALL, WE'D LIKE TO THANK ALL THE **GREAT** GUYS AND GALS AT HOUSTON WITHOUT WHOM **SKYLAB** WOULDN'T HAVE BEEN POSSIBLE!
SCOT
SCOT
TED
THE GROUND CREW WAS BEAUTIFUL, JUST A-OKAY! AND SO WERE ALL THE FOLKS AT DATA CONTROL - ERICH, WILHELM AND HANS! AND SPECIAL THANKS TO CHRIS AND BILL FOR BEING TERRIFIC FLIGHT DIRECTORS!
SCOT
SCOT
TED
WE'D ALSO LIKE TO THANK CONGRESS FOR MAKING **SKYLAB** A REALITY!
RIGHT! AND PRESIDENT NIXON, FOR SUPPORTING US **ALL THE WAY!**
©GBTrudeau
SCOT
SCOT
TED
ALSO, ELLIE AT THE CAR POOL!
YOU'RE FANTASTIC.
ALL OF YOU.
SCOT
SCOT
TED

ZONKER HARRIS?
YEAH... YOU MUST BE MY ATTORNEY..
203
I'VE BEEN TRYING TO REACH YOU ALL WEEK. WHERE HAVE YOU BEEN?
HOME. I ONLY JUST CHECKED IN TODAY.
THE TRIAL'S TOMORROW, HARRIS. WE'VE GOT PRECIOUS LITTLE TIME TO PREPARE A CASE..
SO HOW'S IT LOOK, COUNSELOR? DO I STAND ANY CHANCE AT ALL?
NAH.
SWELL.
GBTrudeau

LADIES AND GENTLEMEN. I HOPE YOU WILL FORGIVE THIS MOST BOTHERSOME FORMALITY OF JURY DUTY.
FORTUNATELY, THE SORDID CASE OF MR. ZONKER HARRIS, AS YOU SHALL SHORTLY SEE, IS A PRETTY SIMPLE AFFAIR.
AS PROSECUTING ATTORNEY, I SHALL PROVE TO YOU, BEYOND A SHADOW OF A DOUBT, THAT THE DEFENDANT IS GUILTY OF TWENTY-TWO COUNTS OF POSSESSION OF MARIJUANA, DEALING IN ILLEGAL DRUGS, AND RESISTING ARREST!
WE SHOULD HAVE YOU OUT OF HERE IN NO TIME.

THOSE SENTIMENTS NOTWITHSTANDING, SIR, THE FACT IS YOU BROKE THE LAW, AND WE MUST...
ZONKER! BABY!
HUH?
MOM! YOU MADE IT!
SORRY I WAS LATE, HONEY!
I MUST ASK YOU, SIR, TO...
HEY, MOM! THIS IS MR. MOSELY, THE D.A.! HE'S PROSECUTING ME!
©B Trudeau
AH.. HELLO, MRS. HARRIS..
BOO! HISS!! THROW THE BUM OUT!

THE PROSECUTION RESTS. THANK YOU, MR. HARRIS. YOUR WITNESS, COUNSELOR...
HMMPH... YES, NOW THEN, MR. HARRIS...
YEAH? YEAH?...
GBTrudeau
AW, WHAT'S THE USE...
HEY!

HEY, MIKE!
WHA?..!
GBTrudeau
SAY... UM.. ZONK. THIS FRAME-UP HAS BEEN A BIG STRAIN ON YOU, HUH?
I'LL SAY, MIKE! YOU KNOW ME- I HATE GRASS! I JUST GET HIGH ON LIFE! AND AMERICA!
WAIT A MINUTE...

MOSELY! GET YOUR TAIL OVER HERE!
MOSELY, DID YOU PLANT THIS MICROPHONE IN THE DEFENDANT'S HOTEL ROOM? BECAUSE IF YOU DID, I'M GOING TO HAVE TO THROW THIS WHOLE CASE OUT OF COURT!
WHAT?! A MIKE IN THE DEFENDANT'S ROOM?! WHY I'M SHOCKED TO LEARN OF THIS THING! TRULY!
GBTrudeau
OKAY, KID, BEAT IT.
THANKS, YOUR HONOR!

JUDGE, I KNOW HOW YOU FEEL ABOUT ILLEGAL TAPS, AND.. I'M.. I'M REALLY SORRY IT HAPPENED..
I GUESS I JUST GOT OVER ZEALOUS IN MY PURSUIT OF A CONVICTION..
I KNOW- I'M A NEW D.A., AND I SHOULDN'T HAVE BLOWN MY FIRST BIG CASE, BUT..
©BTrudeau
YOU HAD IT IN THE BAG, MAN, YOU HAD IT IN THE BAG!
YESSIR..

HELLO?... HEY, HI YA, ZONK!... WHAT?.. NO, JOANIE'S OUT – ONLY B.D. AND I ARE HOME.. WHAT?!.. THROWN OUT OF COURT? TERRIFIC!
HEY, B.D.! ZONKER'S CASE HAS BEEN THROWN OUT OF COURT! HOW ABOUT THAT, HUH?
HE SAYS THAT'S GREAT, MAN, JUST GREAT!
GBTrudeau

CAMPERS, YOU'VE JUST BEEN LISTENING TO YET ANOTHER WBBY EXCLUSIVE-ZONKER HARRIS, THE BUSTED BOPPER, RAPPIN' ON GRASS!
SAY, BUSTED BOPPER, YOU GOT ANY LAST WORDS TO TELL THE FOLKS ON WHAT YOU LEARNED 'BOUT GRASS?
IT MAY OR MAY NOT BE WRONG, BUT IT SURE IS AGAINST THE LAW!
AMEN!

HELLO?.. YES, THIS IS THE PRESIDENT.. WHO?.. MR. BREZHNEV!?... YOU'RE WHERE?.. AT THE AIRPORT?..
GEE, MR. CHAIRMAN, WE DIDN'T EXPECT YOU UNTIL NEXT WEEK! I'M SORRY WE DIDN'T HAVE ANY BANDS OR ANYTHING OUT THERE...
MY APPOINTMENTS SECRETARY MUST HAVE SLIPPED UP OR SOMETHING.. THINGS GET SO HECTIC AROUND HERE SOMETIMES.. IT MUST BE LIKE THAT AT THE KREMLIN, TOO, HUH?.. YEAH.. YEAH.. RIGHT.
WELL, LOOK, LEONID— WHY DON'T YOU GRAB A CAB AND COME ON IN?
GBTrudeau

MR. NIXON, WITHOUT MEANING TO PRY, I AM MOST CURIOUS AS TO HOW YOU'VE MANAGED TO DEAL WITH THE PRESS DURING THIS NASTY PERIOD...
LEONID, I'D BE HAPPY TO SHOW YOU... ZIEGLER!
RON, ANSWER THIS QUESTION: "RON, WILL THE PRESIDENT TESTIFY BEFORE THE SENATE COMMITTEE?"
YESSIR, MR. NIXON?
TO BE RESPONSIVE AT THIS TIME, THOUGH I WILL SIMPLY SAY THAT, AS I SAID-AND THEREFORE THIS IS A REPEAT OF WHAT I SAID PREVIOUSLY-THAT WHICH I AM UNABLE TO OFFER IN RESPONSE IS BASED ON INFORMATION AVAILABLE TO MAKE NO SUCH STATEMENT!
VERY IMPRESSIVE!
WELL, WE LIKE HIM..
GBTrudeau

THIS IS DAN RATHER AT SAN CLEMENTE, A.K.A. "THE WESTERN WHITE HOUSE."
THE SUMMIT TALKS BETWEEN PRESIDENT NIXON AND SOVIET PARTY CHIEF BREZHNEV CONTINUED TODAY AS THE TWO LEADERS SAT OUTSIDE IN THE GARDENS OF THE CALIFORNIA ESTATE.
AT ONE POINT THIS AFTERNOON, MR. BREZHNEV TURNED TO HIS HOST AND INQUIRED WHEREVER DID HE FIND THE FUNDS TO FINANCE AND KEEP UP SUCH A LOVELY HOME!
IT WAS CONSIDERED BY MANY TO BE A LOW POINT IN THE TALKS.
GBTrudeau

GOOD EVENING. PRESIDENT NIXON AND SOVIET CHIEF BREZHNEV ENGAGED IN ANOTHER ROUND OF VIGOROUS TALKS TODAY.
IT WAS LATER ANNOUNCED THAT THEY HAD REACHED AGREEMENT ON A NEW BILATERAL PENAL-REFORM PROGRAM, WITH A MUTUAL EXCHANGE OF PRISONERS.
UNDER THE NEW ACCORD, THE U.S. WILL SEND THE SOVIETS THREE BLACK MILITANTS, FOUR RADICAL PRIESTS, AND FIFTY ASSORTED DRAFT DODGERS.
IN RETURN, THE U.S. WILL RECEIVE FIVE POETS, TWO BALLET DANCERS, AND A NOBEL-PRIZE LAUREATE.

IT'S TRUE! I HEARD IT ON THE RADIO. THEY JUST SIGNED A SPACE ACCORD!
THAT'S INCREDIBLE! OUR ASTRONAUTS AND THE SOVIET COSMONAUTS WORKING TOGETHER!.. WHEN DOES IT GO INTO EFFECT?
IMMEDIATELY!
TERRIFIC!
KNOCK KNOCK!
JUST A SECOND!.. I'M IN THE SHOWER...
USA

TODAY MR. NIXON AND MR. BREZHNEV SIGNED A "DECLARATION OF INTENT" AS AN IMPORTANT PRELUDE TO A FUTURE SALT TREATY.
MEANWHILE, OTHER SOVIET AND AMERICAN OFFICIALS IN NEW YORK WERE HAMMERING OUT AN UNUSUAL CULTURAL ACCORD.
THIS NEWEST AGREEMENT CALLS FOR COLLABORATIVE SPRING PLANNING BETWEEN THE SOVIET AND AMERICAN FASHION INDUSTRIES!
THIS WAS WIDELY VIEWED AS AN AMERICAN CONCESSION.
©B Trudeau

LADIES AND GENTLEMEN— SOVIET PARTY CHIEF **LEONID BREZHNEV!**
GREETINGS, AMERICAN PEOPLE. TONIGHT I WOULD LIKE TO TAKE THE OPPORTUNITY TO TELL YOU HOW MUCH I HAVE ENJOYED MY VISIT TO YOUR COUNTRY.
IN MY TRAVELS, I COULD NOT HELP BUT FALL IN LOVE WITH YOUR WONDERFUL PEOPLE, YOUR WONDERFUL TOWNS, YOUR WONDERFUL VALLEYS AND ORCHARDS, YOUR WONDERFUL WHEAT FIELDS.
PARTICULARLY THE WHEAT FIELDS.

YOU GOT **WHAT?**
A **JOB**, MIKE.. TEMPORARY. I'M GONNA BE A BARTENDER AT "THE JOLLY BEAVER."
WHATEVER FOR?
I GOTTA PAY OFF THE LAWYER WHO DEFENDED ME THIS SUMMER. I OWE HIM 300 CLAMS!
WHEN I DIDN'T PAY HIS BILL RIGHT AWAY, HE CALLED ME UP AND SHOUTED, "LAWYERS HAVE TO MAKE THEIR LIVINGS, TOO, BOY! **PAY UP!**..."
OR?
OR I'LL BE HEARING FROM HIS LAWYER.
GB Trudeau

HEY, HONEY! YOU'RE NEW AROUND HERE! WHAT'S YER NAME?
ZONKER HARRIS.
MINE'S ALICE.. ALICE P. SCHWARTZMAN. I'M A GARMENT WORKER... AND A REGULAR!
'SIDE FROM THAT, I'M JUST AN AGIN' LADY... AS WORN OUT AND RAGGEDY AS AN OL' POT HOLDER... SIGH
GIMME A BEER..
MAY I SEE YOUR I.D., PLEASE, MISS?
HEE, HEE!.. BLESS YOU, DARLIN'.
GB Trudeau

BONKER. I WANNA TELL YOU A STRANGE, TRUE STORY. ONCE THERE WAS A PRETTY LITTLE GIRL WITH SATIN BOWS IN HER HAIR AND DREAMS IN HER HEART...
BUT ONE DAY SHE GREW UP AND FOUND THAT LIFE WAS NOT THE HAPPINESS SHE HAD THOUGHT IT. IT WAS FILLED WITH DESPAIR AND 35 YEARS OF HARD, LONELY WORK.
AND... BONKER... BONKER?
YES, ALICE?
BONKER, THAT LITTLE GIRL WAS ME!
I GUESSED, ALICE.

'NIGHT MISS ALICE!
"MISS ALICE"?.. HEE, HEE.. HONEY, THAT'S GREAT!.. SOUNDS LIKE 3:00 A.M. IN AN OL' MGM DETECTIVE MOVIE. I'M ALICE O'HARA, THE OWNER.. AND YOU'RE.. YOU'RE.. CHARLIE! DIG?
GOT IT.
OKAY, LET'S TAKE IT FROM THE TOP.
GOOD NIGHT, MISS ALICE.
'NIGHT, CHARLIE! LOCK 'ER UP, WILLYA?
GBTrudeau

HAVE YOU KNOWN ALICE LONG, HANK?
ALICE? OH, SURE. ALMOST 30 YEARS NOW...
I GOTTA LOT OF RESPECT FOR THAT GAL. SHE'S SMART, AND HAS REAL STYLE AND DIGNITY. YOU KNOW, I MIGHT EVEN LIKE HER BETTER NOW THAN I DID 30 YEARS AGO!
WHY? WHAT WAS SHE LIKE THEN?
SHE WAS A TEASIN' LITTLE TART.
COME AGAIN?
BUILT, TOO.
GBTrudeau

YOU GUYS BOUGHT ME A BIRTHDAY PRESENT? WHAT IS IT?
WELL OPEN IT UP AND SEE, ALICE.
A BOWLING BALL!
YEP! THAT THERE IS A "PRINCESS TEN-PINS"–THE LIGHTWEIGHT MODEL FOR DAMES!
GOLLY,.. I'VE GOT TO BE THE LUCKIEST BARFLY THIS SIDE OF BROOKLYN..
AW, AIN'T NOTHIN' TOO GOOD FOR OUR ALICE'S BIRTHDAY.
SET 'EM UP, BONKER BABY!
RIGHT ON, YOUR GRACE!

LISSEN, MEN-FOLK, SEEIN' HOW THIS HERE'S MY BIRTH-DAY — WHICH YOU ALL KINDLY REMEMBERED — I WANNA TAKE THE FLOOR TO TELL A STORY, ABOUT ME GROWIN' UP IN NEW YORK..
WHEN I WAS ABOUT 16, I USED TO STAND OUTSIDE THE PLAZA HOTEL AT CHRISTMAS TIME TO WATCH THE DEBUTANTES ARRIVIN'. "HI, GLORIA!" I'D YELL. "HI, WENDY! HI, CONSUELA! HI, CHRISTINA!"... BUT THEY NEVER WAVED BACK..
YEARS LATER, I FINALLY FIGURED OUT THAT SOCIETY AND MONEY DON'T REALLY MEAN "CLASS" AT ALL! THE FOLKS HERE ARE THE ONES WITH THE CLASS. — THEY GOT TIME FOR AN OL' LADY...
BRING ON THE VIOLINS!
HEE HEE!
THAT WAS BEAUTIFUL, ALICE.

WHAT? YOU'RE QUITTING?
GOTTA, ALICE. I'VE GOT FOOTBALL PRACTICE COMIN' UP.
FOOTBALL PRACTICE?! HONEY, I NEVER FIGURED YOU FOR A JOCK!
OH, SURE!..
EVERY DAY I RUN FIVE MILES, SLAM MY BODY INTO TACKLING DUMMIES, AND I CATCH PASSES UNTIL MY HANDS ARE RAW!
DO YOU DEVELOP MORE THAN A ONE BEER THIRST?
ABSOLUTELY!

FELLOW PLAYERS. WHAT I HAVE JUST PASSED AMONGST YOU ARE COPIES OF THE NEW TEAM PLAYBOOK I WROTE OVER THE SUMMER. DO NOT OPEN THEM YET.
THE PLAYS IN YOUR PLAYBOOK, IF EXECUTED PROPERLY, PROVIDE THE KEY TO A WINNING SEASON! DO YOU HEAR ME? A WINNING SEASON!
NOW. USING A NUMBER TWO PENCIL, BREAK THE SEAL ON YOUR PLAYBOOKS.. TURN TO PAGE ONE AND READ SILENTLY WHILE I READ ALOUD.
"THIS PLAYBOOK IS DEDICATED TO BART STARR"
"THIS PLAYBOOK IS DEDICATED TO BART STARR."
GB Trudeau

OKAY, SO YOU ALL WON'T LOSE YOUR NEW PLAYBOOKS, EVERYONE WRITE HIS NAME AND ADDRESS ON THE COVER.
HEY, GOT A PEN?
I FORGOT MINE..
I FORGOT WHERE I LIVE.
AT YOUR FRAT..
B.D., WE DON'T HAVE TO PUT IN OUR MIDDLE NAMES, DO WE?
HEY! ZONK'S REAL NAME IS "WALDEN"!
THAT'S MY ADDRESS, SILLY!
SEE, I JUST HATE MY MIDDLE NAME..
TIME'S UP! HAND IN YOUR BOOKS!

BONKER!
ALICE?
BONKER! YOU SAID I COULD VISIT YOU AT PRACTICE, SO HERE I AM!
SO YOU ARE, ALICE! AND WELCOME!
SAAY!! WHO'S THIS GORGEOUS CREATURE HERE?
THAT'S OUR QUARTER-BACK. I FORGET HIS NAME.
MAY I OFFER YOU A MARGARITA HONEY?
ALICE! THAT'S OUT OF LINE!
GB Trudeau

HATE TO DO THIS TO YOU GUYS, BUT B.D. ORDERED ME TO DRILL YOU ON HIS NEW PLAYS, OKAY?... ZONKER, MY MAN, WHAT'S THE "33-A SPLIT CLEVELAND CLUTCH"?
71
30
IT'S A ROLL-OUT AROUND THE LEFT, RONNIE. THE "CLUTCH" IS TYPICALLY USED IN A LAST QUARTER SITUATION WITH US DOWN BY FIVE.
GO ON..
B.D. PITCHES OUT TO CAL, WHO PROMPTLY GIVES IT BACK, AND B.D. SCRAMBLES THROUGH FOR A TOUCHDOWN JUST AS THE FINAL GUN GOES OFF!!
GOOD. THEN WHAT?
THEN WE ALL HUG HIM AND JUMP UP AND DOWN LIKE IDIOTS.
YOU GOT IT!
GBTrudeau

NOW I TRUST I HAVE IMPRESSED UPON YOU JUST HOW VALUABLE MY PLAYBOOK IS TO US IF WE'RE GONNA HAVE A CHAMPIONSHIP SEASON!
IF IT SHOULD FALL INTO THE HAND OF THE OPPOSITION, WE'D BE **FINISHED!** I HOPE YOU HAVE ALL MEMORIZED MY PRECAUTIONARY RULES! ... **HARRIS!**
CAP'N?
HARRIS, SAY SOME BIG BRUISER HAS CORNERED YOU AND IS ABOUT TO TAKE YOUR PLAYBOOK FROM YOU. **WHAT DO YOU DO?**
I LET HIM MAKE A XEROX OF IT?
YOU **EAT** IT!
OH, YEAH, THAT'S RIGHT..

HARRIS! PUT THAT JOINT OUT!
HARRIS, PUT IT OUT OR YOU'RE OFF THE TEAM! YOU'RE HAVING A BAD EFFECT ON THE REST OF THE GUYS!
IT'S TRUE! ZONKER'S SETTING A TERRIBLE EXAMPLE! I'M.. I'M ABOUT TO SUCCUMB!
ME, TOO! I CAN'T TAKE THE PEER-GROUP PRESSURE ANY LONGER!
71
30
10
©BTrudeau

WHATCHA STARING AT, MIKE?
THE BLACK TABLE. WHY DO THEY ALWAYS SIT BY THEMSELVES?
BECAUSE THEY WANT TO.
I DON'T THINK SO, MARK. I THINK IT'S BECAUSE NO ONE'S MADE ANY EFFORT! UNTIL NOW, THAT IS.
MIKE, YOU'RE NOT GOING TO CAUSE A SCENE, ARE YOU?...
CALL IT WHAT YOU WILL! I'M SITTING WITH THEM. IT'S TIME TO START CARING!
HEADS UP, YOU GUYS!
HOO, BOY...
GBTrudeau

HI. MIKE DOONESBURY'S THE NAME. I COULDN'T HELP WONDERING WHY YOU WERE ALL SITTING TOGETHER OVER HERE!
I FIGURED IT WAS PROBABLY BECAUSE YOU WERE TOO SHY TO COME OVER TO THE OTHER TABLES!
HEE, HEE!
HA! HA! HA! HA! HA!
THAT'S NOT IT, IS IT....
GBTrudeau

MAN, WHY DOESN'T MIKE JUST LEAVE THOSE CATS ALONE?
IT'S HIS GRAND EXPERIMENT IN CULTURAL MOBILITY, MARK.
LOOKS LIKE HE'S RUN OUT OF THINGS TO SAY..
DON'T BET ON IT..
HEY, OL' MARTIN LUTHER KING WAS ONE HECK OF A FELLAH, WASN'T HE?
GBTrudeau

OKAY, MY MAN, I'LL TELL YOU WHY WE KEEP TO OURSELVES! IT'S 'CAUSE WE DON'T WANT TO BE NO PART OF SOMEONE ELSE'S LIBERAL "EDUCATION"!
SURE, MAN, YOU MAKE AN EFFORT, BUT IT'S STONE SELF-SERVIN'! WE DON'T WANT TO BE AN **EXPERIENCE** FOR **NOBODY**!
"ANYBODY."
WHAT?
DOUBLE NEGATIVE.
TAKE A WALK, MAN!

YOU KNOW WHAT I'D LIKE TO KNOW, THOR? I'D LIKE TO KNOW WHAT HAPPENED TO BLACK LEADERSHIP.
WHAT BECAME OF THE BRILLIANT BLACK CAPTAINS AND THEIR REVOLUTIONARY DREAMS OF MOBILIZING THEIR COMMUNITIES AND SHAPING THEIR OWN DESTINIES?
I'LL ASK AROUND.
WELL, GET BACK TO ME ON IT!

WE'RE HERE TALKING TO MRS. LILLIAN CLOW ABOUT WHAT IT WAS LIKE WHEN WE TOOK AWAY HER **CLOROX** FOR A MONTH!.. MRS. CLOW?
AN
JUIL
WELL, THE FIRST DAYS WERE THE WORST. JIMMY'S OVERALLS WOULDN'T WASH CLEAN, AND MY HUSBAND STOPPED COMPLI-MENTING ME ON HIS SOCKS.
PEOPLE KEPT DROPPING BY TO MENTION HOW **DINGY** LITTLE DOROTHY'S DRESS LOOKED! BEFORE LONG I WAS GOING THROUGH WITHDRAWAL! I **NEEDED** MY CLOROX!
GB Trudeau
YES, THERE YOU HAVE IT FROM AN ACTUAL HOUSEWIFE. MRS. CLOW IS **NOT** A PROFESSIONAL T.V. ACTRESS!
NOPE. NOT ME.

ZONKER, I'M MIGHTY GLAD YOU TALKED ME INTO MAKING THIS CAMPING TRIP..
IT'S A **GRAND** OPPORTUNITY! I'M PLANNING TO PUSH MYSELF TO THE **OUTER LIMITS** OF MY ENDURANCE, AND TO NEGOTIATE THE MORAL WILDERNESS OF MY **RELATIONSHIP TO NATURE!**
I'M ALSO HOPING TO GET A LITTLE FISHING IN.
GBTrudeau

CLICK
BRRRRR BRRRR!
NOW THEN, MR. SEGRETTI...
YEAH? YEAH?
AT THIS...
SMASH!
DID YOU BRING THAT CLOCK RADIO!?
WELL, GEE, MIKE, I DIDN'T WANNA MISS ANYTHING..

BLAM!
GREAT SHOT, HARRY! COVER ME WHILE I GO PUT A FEW MORE SLUGS IN HIM!—
ZIP!
HEY! THIS ISN'T A DEER! IT'S JUST A KID!
FORGET IT, HARRY— IT'S JUST SOME KID!

WELL, ANOTHER HALF HOUR AND WE SHOULD BE AT WALDEN.
I THINK I'LL TAKE THE RIDGE TRAIL. I'LL MEET YOU AT HOME..
WHAT?!
YOU CAN'T TAKE THE RIDGE TRAIL ALONE! YOU MIGHT GET LOST! OR BREAK YOUR LEG! OR GET EATEN BY A GIANT PUMA!
HEY, I'LL BE OKAY, ZONKER.
YOU KNOW HOW I WORRY.
GBTrudeau

MAN, DO I FEEL LIKE A FOOL! I'M SO LOST I CAN'T BELIEVE IT!
I SHOULD HAVE BEEN HOME TWO DAYS AGO! WHY ISN'T THERE A SEARCH PARTY OUT HERE LOOKING FOR ME?!
AND WHERE IS ZONKER?! DOESN'T HE EVEN **WONDER** WHAT HAPPENED TO ME?
I WONDER WHAT HAPPENED TO MIKE.
©B Trudeau

HEY! I CAN SEE SOME HIKERS DOWN THERE! I'M SAVED!
HELP!
HEELP!
QUIET, UP THERE!
YEAH, PIPE DOWN, KID!
G.B.Trudeau

LOST? HOW COULD HE HAVE GOTTEN LOST? ALL THE TRAILS ARE CAREFULLY MARKED!
I DON'T KNOW! ALL I KNOW IS THAT HE'S WAY OVERDUE!
LOST! THAT NUMBSKULL!
WE'VE GOT TO REPORT IT TO THE POLICE!
TRUST MIKE TO GET LOST IN HIS OWN BACKYARD!
HOLD ON, MIKEY! HELP'S COMING!
YES, I'D LIKE TO REPORT A MISSING TURKEY.
GBTrudeau

HELLO?!
HEY!
HOW DO? WHO ARE YOU?
BOY, AM I GLAD TO SEE YOU! MY NAME'S MIKE DOONESBURY AND..
OH, NO... I'M NOT LOOKING FOR YOU. I'M INVOLVED IN A LIFE OR DEATH SEARCH FOR A NINE-YEAR-OLD BOY!
OH..
SORRY. HOPE THEY FIND YOU.
YEAH.. THANKS..
©GBTrudeau

HAND ME THOSE GLASSES.. I THINK I SEE SOMETHING!
YUP, THERE'S SOMEBODY DOWN THERE, MR. HARRIS.
WHAT'S HE WEARING?
PINK BERMUDA SHORTS AND HUSH PUPPIES.
THAT'S HIM!
TAKE 'ER DOWN SKY-KING.

HI YA, BUDDY.
MIKE! YOU'RE BACK!
YUP. ZONK FOUND ME... SAY, WHAT'S ALL YOUR STUFF DOING HERE IN MY ROOM?
HUH?
OH, MY STUFF! .. OH, .. WELL .. AH .. SEE... UM, I THOUGHT YOU WERE A GONER! YOU WERE LOST FOR .. AH .. OH ..
THREE DAYS!
THAT ALL? GEE, IT SEEMED LIKE AGES..
GB Trudeau

HOWDY DO, SAPPHIRE!
WHAT NOW?..
GOTTA PRESENT FOR YOU.
I FORGOT TO GIVE IT TO YOU LAST WEEK. IT'S FROM MIKE – A LITTLE TASTE TREAT FOR YOUR BREAKFAST TABLE!
HOW THOUGHTFUL. A DEAD TROUT.
'COURSE, YOU GOTTA CLEAN 'IM FIRST!

BAD NEWS, GENTS! THESE HERE ARE ACADEMICS WARNING LISTS FROM THE DEAN.
"THE FOLLOWING PLAYERS ARE INELIGIBLE FOR FOOTBALL DUE TO UNSATISFACTORY MID-TERM GRADES."
RICARDO ROSE, "SPIKE" BONENBURGER, JEFFY DAVIS, AND... B.D.!
WHAT!? NOT POSSIBLE!
YOU'RE FAILING CERAMICS, MAN.

CERAMICS?! HOW COULD I BE FAILING CERAMICS?!
WELL, I'LL READ YOU THE REPORT FROM YOUR INSTRUCTOR IF YOU WANT..
WHAZZIT SAY?
"CERAMICS 11-A. GRADE: D. STUDENT HAS SHOWN POOR ATTITUDE IN THE FEW CLASSES HE MADE."
"FURTHERMORE, HE HAS SPENT ALL TERM WORKING ON ONLY ONE PROJECT– AN ASHTRAY."
LISTEN, CLASSY ASHTRAYS TAKE TIME!
I AGREE. THIS IS UNREASONABLE.

HOMBRE! WHAT NEWS?
YOU GUYS GOT A QUARTER-BACK AGAIN!
MAGNIFICO! WHAT HAPPENED?
I PULLED AN ALL-NIGHTER. FINISHED MY ASHTRAY AND A SPECIAL PROJECT!
MY INSTRUCTOR TOOK ONE LOOK AT MY PROJECT AND GAVE ME A "B"! HE EVEN CALLED ME A TOP-DRAWER ARTISAN!
WHATCHA MAKE?
A TWO-FOOT TERRA-COTTA BEER MUG!

DEAR MOM, HOW IS EVERYTHING in VIETNAM?
EXCEPT FOR A SMALL ATTEMPTED COUP, LAOS HAS BEEN VERY DULL.
FOR A PROFESSIONAL SOLDIER LIKE MYSELF, LAOS IS NOT SUCH AN INTERESTING ASSIGNMENT.
HOW I WISH I COULD BE HOME VIOLATING THE TRUCE ACCORDS.
GB Trudeau

SO! THIS IS THE FAMOUS "PLAIN OF JARS"! WHAT A THRILL!
YEAH, WELL, KEEP YOUR WITS ABOUT YOU! THERE ARE STILL GOVERNMENT PATROLS IN THESE PARTS ALSO, YOUR ODD C.I.A. AGENT..
OH, AND ONE OTHER THING...
WATCH OUT FOR BOMB CRATERS.
ZIP!
GBTrudeau

I DROPPED BY THE DAY CARE CENTER THIS MORNING.
OH? HOW'S JOANIE DOING?
OKAY, I GUESS.. ALL THE LITTLE GIRLS DOWN THERE HAVE A NEW IDOL..
WHO'S THAT?
B.J. KING, OF COURSE!
HEE, HEE! OF COURSE!
LOVE, NINE!
IT WAS OUT! IT WAS OUT, WASN'T IT MS. CAUCUS?!
TENTATIVE, TENTATIVE!
BOP!
BIP!
POW!

"HOWEVER, IT WASN'T LONG BEFORE THE LITTLE BEAR RETURNED.."
FAIRY TALES
OUT! MY SERVE!
WOP!
FAIRY TALES
BONK!
FAIRY TALES
LET! TAKE ANOTHER!
OKAY.
GBTrudeau

HOWIE, DO YOU KNOW WHO BILLIE JEAN KING IS?
SURE, SILLY!
WELL, WHEN I GROW UP, I'M GOING TO BE A TENNIS PLAYER, JUST LIKE HER!
ME, TOO! ME, TOO! I WANNA GROW UP TO BE A PROFESSIONAL TENNIS PLAYER, JUST LIKE BILLIE JEAN KING!
HOWIE! BREAK-THROUGH!
WHAT? WHAT'D I SAY?
A
12
A

WHO'S THIS?.. ZONKER, HI, HONEY... JOANIE. SAY, WHO'S MAKING DINNER TONIGHT? DO YOU KNOW?..
DOUBLE FAULT!
HEE, HEE!
MIKE?.. OKAY, LOOK WHEN HE COMES IN, COULD YOU TELL HIM I'LL BE LATE FOR DINNER?
DEUCE!
HA, HA!
HEE!
WHAT?.. WELL, I PROMISED LISA I'D HELP HER STRING HER RACQUET... IT MEANS A LOT TO HER, SO..
HEE!
HEE!
WHEE!
HA!
GBTrudeau
WAAAH! NINA GOT CHOCOLATE ON MY TENNIS DRESS!
CRISIS. GOTTA GO.

ELLIE, WHAT'RE **YOU** DOING HERE? I THOUGHT YOU LEFT FOR A TENNIS LESSON!
NO...NOT ME. I'M OFF TENNIS NOW.
OFF TENNIS?! HOW'D **THAT** HAPPEN?
I DUNNO, MS. CAUCUS. IT'S JUST I'VE BEEN THINKING LATELY.
SEE, WE CAN'T **ALL** HAVE BILLIE JEAN AS OUR IDOL. WE WOMEN NEED **DIFFERENT** MODELS. WE CAN'T **ALL** WEAR TENNIS DRESSES WITH BLUE SEQUINS. BASICALLY, IT'S JUST NOT POSSIBLE!
ANYWAY, I'M THINKING OF CHANGING TO MARGARET MEAD.
©GBTrudeau

DID I EVER TELL YOU I ONCE SENT IN AN ARTICLE TO MS. MAGAZINE?
NO..
IT WAS PRETTY SOUL-SEARCHING. I EXPLAINED ALL THE CHANGES I'D GONE THROUGH, HOW MY ATTITUDES TOWARDS WOMEN HAD BEEN IRREVOCABLY ALTERED!
DID IT GET IN?
TO TELL THE TRUTH, I NEVER HEARD FROM THEM.
WHAT?! MAN, YOU'D THINK YOU'D GET THE COURTESY OF A REPLY!
YEAH, WELL, YOU KNOW WOMEN...
YEAH.
GBTrudeau

MARK! WHAT'RE YOU DOING HOME?
HI, DAD! I JUST CAME HOME TO HELP YOU RAKE THE BACKYARD!
GBTrudeau
I BEG YOUR PARDON? YOU CAME HOME TO HELP?
SURE. IT'S A PRETTY BIG JOB, AND I THOUGHT..
YOU WERE EXPELLED.. IS THAT IT? OR JUST SUSPENDED?
HUH?.. OF COURSE NOT! I JUST CAME HOME TO HELP RAKE THE...
IT'S A GIRL, THEN, RIGHT? SOME POOR GIRL...
LEAVES, DAD! TO RAKE THE LEAVES!

MARK, SON, HAVE YOU GIVEN ANY THOUGHT TO THE SORT OF JOB YOU WANT WHEN YOU GRADUATE?
OH, SURE..
I DON'T KNOW WHAT **FIELD** IT'LL BE IN, BUT I KNOW THAT IT WILL HAVE TO BE CREATIVE – A POSITION OF RESPONSIBILITY, BUT NOT ONE THAT RESTRICTS PERSONAL FREEDOM..
IT MUST PAY FAIRLY WELL;.. THE ATMOSPHERE, RELAXED, INFORMAL; MY COLLEAGUES, INTERESTING, MELLOW, AND NOT TOO CONCERNED WITH A STRUCTURED WORKING SITUATION.
IN SHORT, YOU HAVE NO INTENTION OF GETTING A JOB.
I DIDN'T **SAY** THAT.
GBTrudeau

DAD, I DON'T KNOW HOW TO EXPLAIN IT, BUT I WANT A JOB THAT DOESN'T COMPROMISE ME, A JOB I CAN... ENJOY!.
ENJOY?! WHAT'RE YOU TALKING ABOUT, ENJOY?! LIFE IS NOT TO BE ENJOYED, IT'S TO BE GOTTEN ON WITH!
DO YOU THINK I ENJOY MY JOB? NO, I DON'T— I HATE IT, I DESPISE IT! AND ONE DAY YOU'LL HATE YOUR JOB, TOO! ACCEPT IT!
BUT.. DAD...
THAT'S NORMAL, DAMMIT!

MARK, YOU CAN'T AFFORD TO CARRY ON ABOUT BEING COMPROMISED BY MOST JOBS! DO YOU KNOW HOW MUCH IT COSTS JUST TO SURVIVE THESE DAYS?! FOOD, HOUSING, CAR!!..
AND LABOR?! I DON'T EVEN WANT TO TALK ABOUT LABOR!!..
DO YOU HAVE ANY IDEA HOW MUCH IT COST TO HAVE OUR POOL REPAINTED THIS SUMMER?!!
A LOT, RIGHT?
A BUNDLE!
GBTrudeau

MARILOU, HAVE YOU HEARD YOUR SON TALK ABOUT **JOBS** RECENTLY? THE NEW WORD IS THAT WORK IS UNACCEPTABLE UNLESS IT IS "MELLOW," "ENJOYABLE"!
WELL, THERE'S THE LIBERAL ARTS FOR YOU! YOU SEND A KID TO COLLEGE TODAY, AND THEY TEACH HIM TO LOOK FORWARD TO A JOB THAT DOESN'T EXIST!
HAIL THE MIGHTY HUMANITIES! **VIVA** LA ACADEMIA!
YOU'RE GOING TO MISS YOUR TRAIN, DEAR.
I SHOULDA SENT THE LITTLE THUG TO ELECTRICIAN'S SCHOOL.
GBTrudeau

WELL, BASICALLY, SWEETIE, I'M SICK OF **LAOS**! I'VE GOT TWO WEEK'S LEAVE AND I WANT TO GO AS **FAR AWAY** AS I CAN!
FLY
GO!
the lovely UTAH
HERE'S ALL THE MONEY I'VE GOT. WHAT DO YOU SUGGEST?
FLY
GO!
the lovely VERMONT
FLY
GO!
the lovely ASPEN
CAMBODIA.
FLY
GO!
the lovely NEW HAVEN

CAMBODIA?
WHY NOT? TAKE A LOOK AT THIS NEW BROCHURE.
VISIT lovely NEWARK
"COME TO COLORFUL CAMBODIA: A LIVELY, CHANGING COUNTRY, FILLED WITH ALL THE DRAMA OF A NEWLY EVOLVING NATION!"
VISIT lovely BOISE
"THIS FALL, VISITORS WILL BE ABLE TO WITNESS THE SPECTACULAR PAGEANTRY OF A **COMPLETE COMMUNIST TAKEOVER.**"
VISIT lovely SARANAC LK.
A LITTLE COCKY, NO?
YES, I SUPPOSE THAT **IS** A BIT CAVALIER.
VISIT lovely NEW HAVEN
©GBTrudeau

HI, THERE! YOU GOING TO CAMBODIA, TOO?
UH-HUH.
I'M ON A SEVEN-DAY **TEMPLE TOUR!** I'M GOING TO SEE ALL THE OLD HISTORICAL TEMPLES AND MONUMENTS. I'M A NUT FOR THAT SORT OF THING!
GBTrudeau
HA, HA, HA, HA! YOU **FELL** FOR THAT NUMBER?! HEE, HEE, HEE! **EVERYBODY** KNOWS THAT ALL THE HISTORICAL SITES IN CAMBODIA HAVE LONG SINCE BEEN DESTROYED BY BOMBS AND FIRE-FIGHTS!
NO.. **NO**.. MY LIFE'S SAVINGS...
YOU SUCKER!

YES, I'M AFRAID YOUR INFO'S CORRECT, BOSS. MOST OF THESE PLACES WERE DECIMATED.
TOURS
ARE YOU SURE?
CERTAINLY. ANGKOR WAT GOT IT A FEW YEARS AGO. TA PROHM, THE AKYOM STEP PYRAMIDS, THE LATE KHMER BUILDINGS, EVEN THE WESTERN ROYAL TERRACES — ALL OF THESE WERE DESTROYED IN THE WAR...
TOURS
IN FACT, I THINK WE CAN GO TO ONLY A COUPLE OF THE SIGHTS HERE. AND THEY'RE IN THE JUNGLE!
WELL, IF WE'RE GOING INTO THE JUNGLE, I BETTER REST UP. WHERE'S THE HOTEL?
TOURS
I GOT SOME MORE BAD NEWS, BOSS.
I CAN'T STAND IT.
TOURS
GBTrudeau

MONUMENTS! I'M MOSTLY INTERESTED IN MONUMENTS!
YEAH, WELL DON'T GET YOUR HOPES UP. WE'LL BE LUCKY IF WE FIND ANY..
TOUR
IT'S PRETTY WILD COUNTRY, SO I HOPE YOU'RE NOT INCLINED TO GIVIN' IN TO FATIGUE..
TOURS
OH, YEAH – I'M SURE I DON'T HAVE TO REMIND AN OL' TROOPER LIKE YOU...
TOURS
.. BUT WATCH OUT FOR BOMB CRATERS.
TOURS
ZIP!
G.B. Trudeau

THE **MUSEUM**! WHAT HAPPENED TO IT? IT'S.. IT'S TOTALLY **DEMOLISHED**!
I KNOW, BOY, I KNOW! I WAS THE CURATOR.
YOU WRETCHED SOUL! DID THIS HAPPEN DURING THE SECRET BOMBINGS?
SECRET BOMBINGS? BOY, THERE WASN'T ANY **SECRET** ABOUT THEM! **EVERYONE** HERE KNEW! **I** DID, AND MY **WIFE**, SHE KNEW, TOO! SHE WAS WITH ME, AND I REMARKED ON THEM!
I SAID "LOOK, MARTHA, HERE COME THE BOMBS."
IT'S TRUE, HE DID.
GBTrudeau

HEY, BOSS! GET YOUR CAMERA READY! I SEE A SMALL BUT INTACT SHRINE UP AHEAD!
LUCKY DAY!
MAKE HASTE, BOSS! THIS IS A REAL FIND!
YIIIPEEE!
BOOM!!
TOO LATE..
RATS! RATS! RATS!

YOU KNOW, BOSS, I JUST THOUGHT OF SOMETHING YOU COULD SEE - MY ALMA MATER, THE LOCAL UNIVERSITY!
YOU WENT TO COLLEGE?
FOR A WHILE. I DROPPED OUT, THOUGH.. I GOT REALLY TURNED OFF TO IT.
HOW COME?
I DUNNO - JUST A WEIRD PLACE. LIKE ONCE WE HAD THIS ANTI-WAR SIT-IN, SO THEY SENT IN A COMPANY OF TROOPS WHO CLOSED THE SCHOOL DOWN AND EXECUTED THE ENTIRE FRESHMAN CLASS!
LOST A LOT OF GOOD FRAT PLEDGES THAT YEAR..
I'LL BET.
GBTrudeau

THERE YOU HAVE IT, BOSS. 300,000 WAR VICTIMS!
WOW! I CAN'T BELIEVE IT!
WELL, THIS IS THE BIGGEST IN ALL OF CAMBODIA.
I'M AMAZED! AND I'M NO STRANGER TO REFUGEE CAMPS!
TOURS
EVEN THE CAMBODIANS ARE INCREDULOUS – FOLKS COME OUT HERE ALL THE TIME JUST TO SEE THE CAMP! IT'S CONSIDERED AN IMPORTANT SITE!
I JUST HOPE IT DOESN'T GET ALL TOURISTY.
GBTrudeau

MAN, JUST SEEING THE CONDITIONS HERE IS REALLY GETTING TO ME.. IT'S JUST NOT FAIR! SOMEONE SHOULD TAKE THE RESPONSIBILITY FOR VICTIMIZING ALL THESE PEOPLE!
TOURS
YOU KNOW, IF WE COULD GET SOME OF THESE REFUGEES OVER TO WASHINGTON, WHERE THEY COULD.. ..WELL.. LOBBY ON THEIR OWN BEHALF, I BET WE'D GET SOME ACTION THEN!
YEAH!
YOU GOT ANY IDEA HOW WE COULD GET 'EM OVER?
COME TO THINK OF IT, BOSS, I KNOW A LOCAL AUSSIE PILOT WHO OWES ME A FAVOR!
THEN IT'S DECIDED!
OKAY, LISTEN UP, PEOPLE!
TOURS
GBTrudeau

MY FELLOW SOUTH-EAST ASIANS! THE TIME HAS COME TO FIGHT BACK AGAINST YOUR WOEFUL LOT IN LIFE!
LET US GO TO WASHINGTON, D.C., TO PUT YOUR CASE BEFORE THE U.S. CONGRESS, TO HOLD IT ACCOUNTABLE FOR THE AIR-WAR POLICIES WHICH HAVE CAUSED YOUR MISERABLE CONDITION!
YES, WE MUST LOBBY FOR YOUR RECONSTRUCTION! I WANT EACH REFUGEE HERE TO PICK ONE CONGRESSMAN OR SENATOR TO SPEAK TO!
GBTrudeau
I DIBS HOWARD BAKER!
CARL ALBERT!
I WANT THE LITTLE JAP!
ONE AT A TIME, ONE AT A TIME!

WELL, LIVINGSTON, CAN YOU FIGURE OUT HOW TO GET THESE FOLKS TO WASHINGTON? FRANKLY, WE'RE STUMPED..
7621
WELL, I'VE BEEN THINKING, FELLOWS. I'M DUE TO TAKE BACK A SHIPMENT OF 200,000 EMPTY COKE BOTTLES. I SUPPOSE WE COULD DUMP 'EM, AND PUT YOUR REFUGEE FRIENDS IN THE PACKING CASES.
GBTrudeau
HMM.. SOUNDS GOOD TO ME..
UNLESS, OF COURSE, THEY OBJECT TO BEING STUFFED INTO SMALL WOODEN CRATES..
NOT AT ALL. THAT'S WHAT THEY LIVE IN NOW.
FINE! THEN WE LEAVE AT DAWN!

EVERYBODY LOADED?
YUP, THIS IS THE LAST CRATE.
CONTENT EMPTY BOTTLE
GOOD MORNING. THIS IS YOUR CAPTAIN, LIVINGSTON PLIMPTON, SPEAKING. I'D LIKE TO WELCOME YOU ABOARD FLIGHT 505 TO WASHINGTON, D.C., WITH FUEL STOPS IN HONOLULU AND L.A.!
SHOULD YOU REQUIRE ANY SERVICE – LIQUID REFRESHMENT, LARGER AIR HOLES – JUST RAP ON YOUR BOX, AND FLIGHT ATTENDANT PHRED WILL HELP YOU OUT. OTHERWISE, HAVE A **NICE FLIGHT!**
SEAT BELTS, EVERYBODY!
CLICK!
CLICK!
CLICK!
CLICK!
GB Trudeau

IT
WAAH!
HEY! WHAT'S THAT?
NTS
CONTENTS: EMPTY BOTTLES
PROP of CocaC
EVERYTHING OKAY IN HERE?.. AWW... HEY... BEAUTIFUL. CONGRATULATIONS, PEOPLE.
ANOTHER LITTLE COKE BOTTLE HAS JUST COME INTO THE WORLD!
GBTrudeau
GOOCHIE, GOOCHIE!
SIGH SOME LOBBY...

HI!
HI, PHRED. EVERYTHING QUIET BACK THERE?
OH, SURE. ALL GOES WELL. I JUST FINISHED BRIEFING EVERYBODY. IF AND WHEN YOU GET US THROUGH CUSTOMS, WE'RE ALL GOING TO MEET DOWNTOWN AT THE CAPITOL.
I HOPE IT ALL WORKS OUT. FRANKLY, I'M A LITTLE BIT WORRIED — I DON'T KNOW A SOUL THERE, AND I HAVE NO IDEA WHERE WE'RE ALL GOING TO STAY..
ARE THERE ANY GOOD REFUGEE CAMPS IN THE WASHINGTON AREA?
HMM... LEMME THINK..
GBTrudeau

EMPTY COKE BOTTLES, I **SWEAR** IT! I'M **VERY** CONCERNED ABOUT CAMBODIA'S ECOLOGY!
OKAY, OKAY! YOU'RE FREE TO GO.
U.S. CUSTOMS
EMPTY COKE BOTTLES.. HEH! IMAGINE!
CONTEN
EMPTY
U.S. CUSTOMS
IT'S THE REEAL THING!
U.S. CUSTOMS
HEE, HEE!
ARE WE THERE YET? ARE WE THERE?
I SEE NOTHING, **NOOOTHING!**
BUMP!
BUMP!
U.S. CUSTOMS
GBTrudeau

...AND SENATOR MANSFIELD CALLED EARLIER. HE WANTS TO KNOW WHEN YOU'RE GOING TO HAVE YOUR NEW FARM BILL FINISHED.
GBTrudeau
AND MAYOR WILLS CALLED. HE SAYS HE ASKED YOU TO SPEAK AT THE ROTARY, BUT YOU STILL HAVEN'T TOLD...
I KNOW, I KNOW, **I KNOW!**
JOHN, WILLYA JUST KEEP THESE PEOPLE OFF MY BACK FOR THE REST OF TODAY!? MY ULCERS ARE **KILLING** ME, AND IF I HAVE **ONE MORE** AGGRAVATION, I'M GOING TO..
EXCUSE ME, SENATOR— THERE ARE 300 CAMBODIAN REFUGEES HERE TO SEE YOU.

300 CAMBODIAN REFUGEES!?
THAT'S RIGHT, GEORGE. THEY'RE IN MY OFFICE RIGHT NOW, BUT THEY'VE GOT NO PLACE AT ALL TO STAY...
WE'RE GONNA LOOK PRETTY BAD IN THE PRESS IF WE DON'T DO SOMETHING FOR THEM, GEORGE. WE CAN'T VERY WELL HAVE THEM CAMPING OUT ON THE STEPS OF THE CAPITOL, CAN WE?
ANYWAY, I THOUGHT IF ALL OF US ON THE FOREIGN RELATIONS COMMITTEE PITCHED IN AND TOOK ON A COUPLE DOZEN REFUGEES AS HOUSEGUESTS, WE MIGHT BE ABLE TO SAVE THE SITUATION.
WELL... LEMME CALL MY WIFE.
I KNEW I COULD COUNT ON YOU, GEORGE!
GBTrudeau

THIS WEEK IN THE CAPITAL, THERE'S A VERY HAPPY DEVELOPMENT IN THE SAGA OF THE CAMBODIAN REFUGEES.
THE REPORT FROM WASHINGTON IS THAT LEADING CITIZENS HAVE OPENED UP THEIR HEARTS AND THEIR TOWN-HOUSES TO THE SCRAPPY LITTLE WAR VICTIMS.
ALL OVER GEORGE-TOWN, THE CAMBODIANS HAVE FOUND REFUGE WITH THE FAMILIES OF RANKING CONGRESSMEN, SENATORS, AND GOVERNMENT OFFICIALS!
WILL MINUTE RICE BE OKAY?
I DON'T KNOW WHY NOT.

OKAY, FELLAHS, YOU'LL BE THE LAST ONES TO GO..
NOW REMEMBER, IT'S VERY IMPORTANT THAT YOU MAKE A GOOD IMPRESSION. TRY TO BE POLITE, SMILE A LOT, AND DON'T GET INTO ANY ARGUMENTS.
HEY, BOSS! SENATOR TUNNEY ON THE PHONE!
TELL HIM ALL WE GOT LEFT ARE THREE VILLAGE ELDERS AND A WAR ORPHAN!
HE SAYS HE'LL TAKE 'EM!
OKAY, NOW I'M COUNTING ON YOU GUYS..
©BTrudeau

MILLIE, DID YOU HEAR THE JACKSONS WERE ABLE TO GET A REFUGEE?
MOI AUSSI, MY DEAR.
OH, C'MON, MILLIE, I DON'T BELIEVE YOU..
SEE FOR YOURSELF. HE'S IN HERE HAVING BREAKFAST.
MILLIE! YOU DID GET A REFUGEE! FOR REAL!
YOU LUCKY STIFF!
YOU BETTER BELIEVE IT, TOOTS!

ADMIRAL, I'D LIKE YOU TO MEET LOL NOL TOL, MY REFUGEE HOUSEGUEST! HE WAS A LITTLE HUNGRY, SO HE STARTED DINNER EARLY..
WELL, I'VE GOT TO SEAT THE OTHER GUESTS, SO I'LL JUST LEAVE YOU TWO TO GET ACQUAINTED!
CAN I HAVE YOUR ROLL?

WELL, I THINK WE SHOULD BE TESTIFYING ANY DAY NOW!
YOU THINK SO, BOSS?
SURE! HOW ARE THE ENGLISH LESSONS COMING?
UH... WELL, I...
"AS WE RECALLS IT, MAYBE!"
"EXCUSE, BUT WHERE ARE H.E.W.?"
"EXECUTIVE PLIVILEGE!"
"STOP IT, SENATOR!"
"HOW WAS THE SON OF YOUR MOTHER?"
FRANKLY, BOSS, I'M WORRIED.
"VOTE YOU ELASTIC PIPELINE?"
FAR OUT...

NO PROBLEM, MIKE— THE COMMITTEE WILL HEAR THE REFUGEES!
REALLY?
YUP. I SPOKE TO THE CHAIRMAN, AND WHEN I EXPLAINED THAT ALL 300 OF THEM HAD TURNED UP AT YOUR OFFICE THIS MORNING, HE AGREED TO HOLD THE HEARINGS THIS AFTER-NOON.
WHEW... WHAT A RELIEF.. YOU HAVE NO IDEA...
WHERE ARE THEY NOW?
MY SECRETARY TOOK THEM OVER TO MACDONALD'S FOR LUNCH.
©GBTrudeau

STATE YOUR NAME AND OCCUPATION, PLEASE.
MY NAME IS **PHRED.** I'M AN INSURGENT FOR THE PATHET LAO, CURRENTLY ON FURLOUGH. I'M A NATIVE OF HUÉ, VIETNAM.
AND THE GENTLEMAN NEXT TO YOU?
I'M HIS DISTINGUISHED COUNSEL.

I AM AN OLD WOMAN, SIRS. I KNOW NOTHING OF POLITICS. I KNOW ONLY THAT THE AIRPLANE CAME AND DESTROYED MY VILLAGE.
BUT CAN YOU BE SURE IT WAS AN AMERICAN PLANE, MS. LOO? THIS, OF COURSE, IS OF VITAL IMPORTANCE!
YOU SEE, MS. LOO, THERE ARE MANY DIFFERENT KINDS OF PLANES — THERE ARE BIG ONES, LITTLE ONES, JET PLANES AND..
IT WAS A NAVY McDONNELL F4B-1 PHANTOM II.
OH, YES, THAT'S OURS.
GBTrudeau

MR. PHRED, THE COMMITTEE WOULD LIKE TO THANK YOU FOR ORGANIZING SO EFFECTIVELY ALL THE TESTIMONY WE HAVE HEARD TO DATE.
NOW THEN, HAVE YOU ITEMIZED THOSE MEASURES YOU DEEM NECESSARY FOR A SHORT-TERM CESSATION OF THE SUFFERING OF SOUTHEAST ASIAN REFUGEES?
YES, SENATOR. COUNSEL AND I HAVE PREPARED A LIST OF WHAT WE FEEL ARE THE MINIMAL MATERIALS REQUIRED TO ALLEVIATE THE CURRENT CRISIS..
PROCEED.
3.5 MILLION SLEEPING BAGS...
HOLD IT.

THE COMMITTEE WOULD LIKE TO THANK THE REFUGEE WITNESSES FOR THEIR MANY IN-SIGHTS INTO THE REFUGEE PROBLEM IN SOUTHEAST ASIA.
WE APPRECIATE THE TROUBLE YOU TOOK TO COME ALL THE WAY TO WASHINGTON, D.C. TO PROVIDE YOUR TESTIMONY.
ALL IN ALL, YOU'VE BEEN **GREAT** SPORTS, EVERY ONE OF YOU! I MEAN IT!
©B Trudeau
WHAT DO WE HAVE FOR THE WITNESSES, JOHNNIE?
WELL, SENATOR, FOR THE LADIES, FROM SPEIDEL, THE **LATEST** IN **WATCHBANDS!**

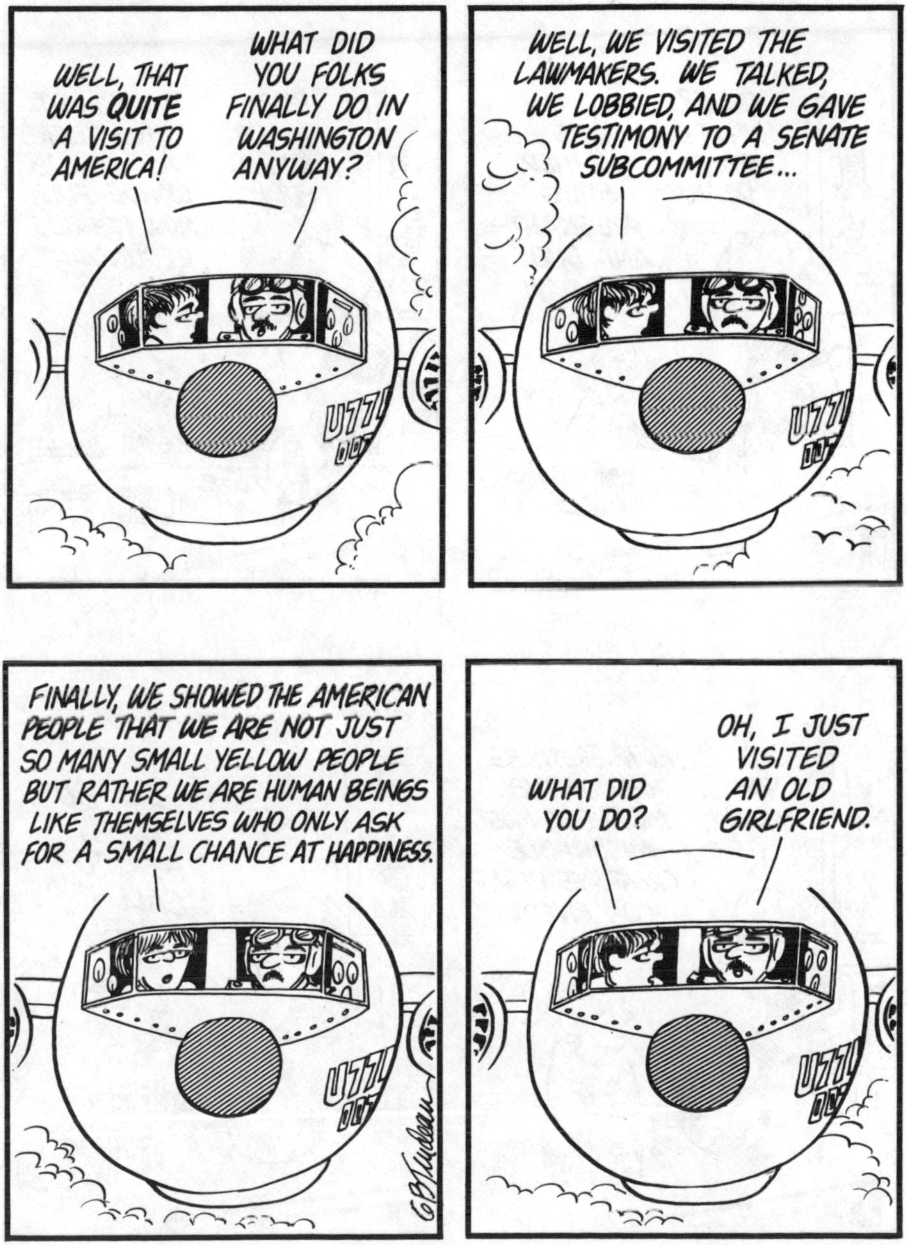
WELL, THAT WAS QUITE A VISIT TO AMERICA!
WHAT DID YOU FOLKS FINALLY DO IN WASHINGTON ANYWAY?
WELL, WE VISITED THE LAWMAKERS. WE TALKED, WE LOBBIED, AND WE GAVE TESTIMONY TO A SENATE SUBCOMMITTEE...
FINALLY, WE SHOWED THE AMERICAN PEOPLE THAT WE ARE NOT JUST SO MANY SMALL YELLOW PEOPLE BUT RATHER WE ARE HUMAN BEINGS LIKE THEMSELVES WHO ONLY ASK FOR A SMALL CHANCE AT HAPPINESS.
WHAT DID YOU DO?
OH, I JUST VISITED AN OLD GIRLFRIEND.
GBTrudeau

ELLIE?.. WHAT'S WRONG, DEAR?
IT'S MOTHER... SHE'S PREGNANT— AND DUE ANY DAY!
BUT.. THAT'S WONDER-FUL!..
NO, IT'S NOT. FIVE YEARS AGO IT WAS WONDERFUL. NOW IT'S JUST REDUNDANT.
YOU MEAN..
FOUR BROTHERS. FOUR OF THE MEANEST, MOST MISERABLE CREATURES EVER CONCEIVED!
OH DEAR...
I'VE GOT TO GET HER TO CALL IT OFF!
©BTrudeau

GOODNESS KNOWS I TRIED TO TELL HER, JEAN! "MOMMY" I SAID, "WHAT'S WITH ALL THE BABIES? YOU WANT TO BE A HOUSE-WIFE ALL YOUR LIFE?"
USC
BUT SHE KEEPS TURNIN' 'EM OUT! EVERY YEAR, JUST LIKE CLOCKWORK! IT'S REALLY AMAZING!
USC
I DUNNO.. MAYBE I'LL JUST HAVE TO WORK ON MY FATHER INSTEAD..
USC
AS I UNDERSTAND IT, HE FIGURES HEAVILY IN ALL THIS..
OH, YEAH?
USC
GBTrudeau

MOMMY GOES INTO THE HOSPITAL TODAY. I GUESS I BETTER START THINKING POSITIVELY ABOUT MY NEWEST SIBLING..
GOOD IDEA, DEAR!
I JUST HOPE IT'S A SISTER. I NEED A SISTER!
GBTrudeau
ALSO, IT'S MORE "IN" TO BE A FEMALE THAN A MALE THESE DAYS! MUCH MORE FASHIONABLE.
IT IS?
SURE!
I DON'T THINK THERE'S ANY QUESTION ABOUT IT...
IT'S TRUE. I READ IT IN "TIME" LAST WEEK.

ELLIE! PHONE FOR YOU, DEAR!
HELLO?.. HI, DADDY!.. SHE DID? WHAT IS IT?!
IT'S A WOMAN!
"WOMAN"?
IT'S A BABY WOMAN!

SAY, THOR, DO YOU KNOW ANYTHING ABOUT THIS CHRISTMAS ROCK-PAGEANT SCOT'S PLANNING?
OH, SURE. IT'S REALLY SHAPIN' UP...
HE'S GOT ABOUT THIRTY NEIGHBORHOOD PEOPLE PARTICIPATING — MUSICIANS, ACTORS, LIGHT PEOPLE — YOU NAME IT!.. I MYSELF PLAY JOSEPH IN THE NATIVITY SCENE..
JOSEPH? YOU?!
YEAH, WELL, AT FIRST I REFUSED TO DO IT... BUT THEN I CHECKED OUT MARY AT THE REHEARSAL TODAY.
CUTE?
I'M TELLIN' YA — THE FOXIEST IN TOWN!
GBTrudeau

WHERE'S THE SECOND WISE MAN?! THAT CHORD WAS HIS **CUE!**
SORRY, REV! I COULDN'T FIND MY CROWN...
C'MON, MAN, GET IT TOGETHER! JOSEPH, TAKE IT FROM THE TOP AGAIN! LET'S GET IT **RIGHT!**
GBTrudeau
LOOK, MARY, ANOTHER MAGUS COMETH!
NOW HIT IT! **HIT IT!**
MYRRH IS MINE, A BITTER PERFUME!!
GOOD! GOOD!

WHAT IS IT, THOR?
DIRECTOR, I DON'T WANT TO BE JOSEPH ANYMORE...
WHY NOT, THOR? IT'S A MAJOR ROLE, YOU KNOW..
YEAH, BUT HE'S BORING! THERE'S NO CHARACTER DEVELOPMENT..
STILL, HE'S VERY KEY TO THE PAGEANT.
LOOK, HOW ABOUT IF YOU JUST RE-CAST ME AS A NUBIAN SLAVE?
IN THIS DAY AND AGE?
OKAY, THEN— A NUBIAN WAITER!
GBTrudeau

NO! NO! NO! NO!
WHAT'S THE PROBLEM, REV?
WHAT'S THE PROBLEM?! HAVEN'T YOU PEOPLE EVEN LOOKED AT THE SCRIPT?!
FOR THE LAST TIME, THE SECOND SHEPHERD DOES NOT LAY DOWN THE RHYTHM GUITAR RIFF UNTIL AFTER THE VISITATION!
I THOUGHT THE INN-KEEPER WAS PLAYING RHYTHM..
NO, VIBES.
I CAN'T BELIEVE WE OPEN TOMORROW..
GBTrudeau

GOOD EVENING, AND WELCOME TO THIS YEAR'S CHRISTMAS ROCK-PAGEANT.
IN OUR SHOW TONIGHT, MARY IS PLAYED BY SCARLET ZUCKERMAN AND JOSEPH IS THOR JACKSON.
THE SHEPHERDS ARE PLAYED BY CHICO, ANDY AND NICK, AND THE INNKEEPER AND HIS WIFE ARE TIM AND MARGOT BIXBY.
THE PART OF BABY JESUS IS PLAYED BY A HIDDEN 40-WATT LIGHT BULB.
©GBTrudeau